CLARITY OF THE HEART
© 2012 by Don Glass

A book of Spiritually motivational poetry and prose

ISBN 978-0-9826031-0-9

Published by:

Don Glass
Winners Unlimited Publishing Co.

'Clarity of The Heart' can be ordered online through my website, which is www.donglass.com. If you would like an autographed copy or more than one autographed copy, I have an email address at my website. If you email me, I will send you the details via reply email. Since I am now a senior citizen and do not know when our Creator will take me, this option is valid only while I am still physically on this planet, and while I am able to sign my name.

ACKNOWLEDGEMENTS

I have been working on this poetry/prose book on and off since 1977, and there have been many people who have helped and inspired me along the way. However, the most notable people along the way were the members of the Unity Pyramid Singles Group in Houston in 1977, Molly Khan, Sharon Thomas, Robin Shrader, Raylene Parsons, Mary Wagoner, Reverend John Rankin, and Reverends Sig and Jane Paulson (deceased). For others I do not remember, please forgive my aging memory.

FOREWORD

This is a relatively long Foreword, but is essential to read for an adequate understanding of the rest of this book. You will soon see that it is time and effort well invested.

Early in my life I would not have considered being an author of a poetry/prose book. In fact, I thought I was going to be an engineer, or possibly a computer programmer. As a young man I did mostly sales work, which in part, led me to computer programming. So I did become a computer programmer, but as a young man, I had no inkling that I would become an author.

In October 1976, my second wife and I had recently separated, and I was in great emotional pain as a result since I dearly loved her. The depth of my sorrow and despair was immeasurable, and one evening while alone, I really wanted to die. Instead, I became sufficiently motivated and willing to feel those feelings because I chose to live. And to continue resisting such strong feelings would have been to choose denial of my real inner self which would have likely led to the death of my physical body at that point since I was in such intense pain; i.e. I could have easily chosen to take my life. The release and awareness of the pain was as much as I could bear, and was truly an extremely deep gut-wrenching experience that probably only lasted a few minutes, but seemed like an eternity of pain because of the extreme intensity. I believe it was as much emotional pain as any person can feel at one time and still live. Release of pain that intense meant gut-wrenching crying, and my face was awash with my tears. I was connecting with the pain of a nice marriage ending and internally correlating that with the events and my states of mind that had brought me to that point; i.e. I was trying very hard to understand the cause of my failed marriages. Although I had tried hard to understand it intellectually prior to that time, I could not, and it was at that point of connecting and experiencing the genuine source of my pain and problems that I got major relief and a deep spiritual healing experience. The connection to the past, especially of my childhood, became the focus in my heart and mind, and I began to understand how the unhealed emotional imprints from my childhood were the source of the failure of my two marriages and other unhappy outcomes in my life.

After the awesome release of pain, I sat there amazed at the experience that I had just gone through, knowing that it was the right thing for me to have done to attain some much needed emotional healing. Each passing second after that was a transition of moving from the pain of the experience to a strongly increasing joyful loving experience. It was like a veil over my mind had been lifted. Almost infinite amounts of information seemed to come to me instantaneously, and I realized that I was remembering these vast quantities of information now that the veil was lifted that was hiding all of this knowledge from myself. I discovered that this was information I already knew, but forgot due to significant amounts of trauma that I had in childhood that subtly had little by little drawn the illusionary veil of unknowing over my conscious-awareness.

As I continued through this experience, I couldn't help but notice that I began to experience a joyful glowing feeling that seemed to be growing by the second. And then I noticed that I was starting to have the experience of unconditional love, something I had only experienced from my paternal grandmother in childhood. But this was huge and unlimited. Soon I began experiencing a non-verbal communication, and instantly I knew that this was from The Holy Spirit (i.e. the connection to our Creator). The communication was crystal clear, such that there was not even one small misunderstanding in our messages to each other. And the communication was faster than lightning; large volumes of information came to me instantaneously and with no feeling of being overloaded. So many beautiful things were communicated to me, the most notable being that the Source of The Universe is unconditionally loving, and wants only what is best for each of His children. Another important Truth is that He created a Universe of Cause and Effect, and that everything in The Universe is made by Him and He is Omnipresent in every part of The Universe, and that He is, in fact, The Universe. And that is how and why He is Omniscient and Omnipotent. I discovered that there is no thought or feeling that I have that He does not know about in advance, even if I am temporarily unaware of it. And because of that, He knows deeply about each individual's real love and faith; and that when a person has real love and faith, that He can be in a bilateral love union with that individual, and that miracles can begin to happen. And when more than one person is joined in that union with common purpose, the possibility and scope of the miracles can be exponentially magnified. Since He is omnipotent, He can transcend normal cause and effect laws at will and do a divine intervention.

    He revealed to me that since He loves all of His creations unconditionally, He could never create 'Hell', nor could He allow 'Hell' to be real and exist. After all, Jesus said that "The Kingdom of Heaven is within you"; he did not say the torture of 'Hell' is within you, nor would he because 'Hell' is not real except for the illusion of it in our own minds. He strongly stated that any religion that teaches that there is a 'Hell' is indeed teaching fear, and misguiding people away from His divine sanctity of unconditional Love and Faith; and that unconditional Love and Faith is the mental and spiritual state that is the natural path to the harvest of His miracles and joy. However, since He loves each of us unconditionally, He gives each of us power of choice, that He would not intervene with our choices, but allow each of us to create whatever we choose, including our own experience of 'Hell' while in a physical body in this world or Universe. He knows that in time, we will learn from our errors and bad choices, and correct them. And He adamantly proclaimed that our souls are the only part of each of us that is real, and are eternally indestructible; and we will go from lifetime to lifetime until we learn to unconditionally love, after which our souls will eternally be in Heaven, a state of mind and being we never really left. As a corollary to 'Hell' not existing and not being real, Satan does not exist, but worldly temptations and people with temporarily evil states of mind exist that would support the belief that we are unfree and deserve to suffer due to the will of some illusory evil supernatural and super-powerful entity. He told me that the cause of much human suffering is humanity's misuse of free will, and because of total investment of belief in only the physical world, many people do not understand true power, and blindly misuse worldly power, which is temporarily a very costly illusion. Thus it is not our Creator that causes the human suffering in the world; it is human misuse of free will.

He revealed to me that since He is Omnipresent, Omniscient, and Omnipotent that He is the only Creator, and that any religion that does not teach that is teaching their people falsities, and their experience of life will be limited in some very important ways. He has revealed to me that there have been many incorrect translations of the original writings of The Bible distorted by the religious beliefs and prejudices of the translators, and that has misled people to dire consequence. In addition, He tells me that much of the text in The Bible has been literally interpreted even though the writing of much of it was intended to be metaphorical and/or symbolic. Also, there are colloquialisms that often change the meanings of important words in just one century, and here we are dealing with about 20 centuries for much of the New Testament, and around 30 centuries for much of the Old Testament. These too, have misled many people to dire consequence, and He wants us to choose to interpret it correctly with His inner guidance. He told me that other religious guidance books have similar problems, and that any disagreement, fight, or war over religion is totally needless since they are about misunderstanding His true nature. He adamantly does not want us fighting these very destructive and needless battles mentally, emotionally or physically. After all, most people are really worshiping the one and only God, and the experience of His Love is grander, more empowering, and more beautiful than anyone can possibly imagine, and once you have a deep experience of Him, you will likely feel His Presence and His Love forever within you since He is always there within each of us. So humanity has really been fighting about nothing, and we can choose to be aware of our common religious beliefs and be at peace for the remainder of time. Why don't we simply choose to do that?

He told me that time is an illusion similar to how the rest of the physical universe is an illusion, and the eternal now is all that there really is. He had to add time to The Universe since we need chronological order in order to function in the illusory physical realm.

There are huge positive ramifications for humanity when enough people choose to 'see The Light' and truly experience and understand the meanings of what I have communicated above. On our current course, we are polluting and destroying our planet, and life around us to the point that many species are becoming extinct more quickly than any phase of human history, and as a result, it is questionable if humanity will survive at all, and if we do, what kind of quality of life are we leaving for our descendants? If enough people come around to The Truths of their inner selves and make a real connection with our Creator soon, then we have a good chance of making it with a very nice quality of life for all people. Each day that this choice is delayed contributes to increasingly larger negative ramifications, and all living beings are paying the price, and will pay a much heavier price as time passes if inadequate action is taken.

This spiritual awakening that I have described is truly the process of forgiveness, and has changed my life for the better in many ways. I would have questioned that my spiritual awakening was real, and possibly concluded that my experience was an illusion of my mind stemming from emotional desperation, but I was left with the awareness of His loving presence and His gentle and loving guidance. I have found that His guidance is not only a strong foundation to depend upon, but if I don't follow His guidance, I always regret it. Not because He is telling me what to do, but because He has unconditional love for me (and all of us) and wants my (and everyone's) life to go without needless difficulties and problems. When I follow His guidance, even though at the time it might appear to be illogical or ridiculous, I am always glad that I did. There have been many times when getting from one place to another in my car or van that He has guided me to take a different path. I would invariably find out later that there was something ahead that would have stopped me or slowed me down considerably for quite a while had I continued to go the path I was taking. He has often guided me in what to say at critical or important times in my life, and has made a positive difference in the outcome of many situations for me. He guides me in every aspect of my life, and always gives me a much better outcome than I would have chosen for myself. My conclusion is that although He does not present Himself with a single physical appearance, He is more real, more powerful, and more unconditionally loving than anything in this whole universe.

It was about a year after that experience that my mind and heart had integrated that experience into everyday life, and poetry began to spontaneously come into my mind. I would often have to find pen and paper, and begin writing it down. I am clear that The Holy Spirit has guided me to write this book. But due to the need to earn money and support myself, I would have to return to the business world, leave the inner world of poetic creativity, and have to unconsciously put on the veil of unknowing temporarily so that I could fulfill the analytical and intellectual demands of business and earning a living in what has often been emotionally harsh and rigid working environments. So it has taken me a long time to get this book written.

My pure intent for writing this book is to make as huge as possible positive difference in as many people's lives as possible. If it makes a significantly positive difference in only one person's life, it will have been worth it. This book is for everyone because its messages, when implemented, can realistically make a huge difference in each individual's life, and in the world.

You can read the poems and prose in this book in any order you choose, of course. However, you will gain the maximum benefit by doing your first reading in the order that they are in the book. After the first comprehensive reading, read any poem or prose you are internally guided to read.

Several words in this book are not in the dictionary, but will make more sense left as is. A good example is the word 'unforgiveness'. The closest word to this in the Webster's dictionary is 'unforgivingness'. This does not make much sense since the opposite meaning of 'forgiveness' would be the best meaning desired to make a point. The word 'unforgivingness' just doesn't get the job done if you look at the definitions. I see it as a minor incompletion or flaw in the development of the English language. So, this type of wording is desirable and used in the messages of this book because of their common sense meanings.

Throughout this book, I have made most poems rhyme, but not always. I am much more concerned with getting the extremely important messages clearly communicated to you. In addition, I have been unconcerned with the rhythm of the words, i.e. for example, I have not gone to any effort to make sure there are the same # of syllables for each matching line. Again, I am much more focused on making the all-important messages clear and getting them to as many people as possible, for there is great urgency for humanity to get these meanings and apply them to their lives.

Please do not rush or try to 'speed read' these poems and prose writings. Slow down and take your time to really digest and understand them to the best of your ability. Much of this book will touch your heart and soul, and you will want to think and reflect so that the messages will be personally meaningful to you, and so you will gain the maximum benefit from the deep meanings. Each time I edited these poems to make them 'book ready', I found myself feeling uplifted and very positive, and I suspect that most of you will have a similar experience. Your life will likely move forward in leaps and bounds from reading this book if you are open to and want that for your life.

I created the design of the book cover according to The Holy Spirit's instructions. The main point The Holy Spirit wanted me to communicate to my readers is that there is no limit to the power of The Holy Spirit, even if many people do not currently believe that is true. Their belief about that will change someday as time passes, for every person will experience this Truth when they are truly ready. Further clarification is necessary for my readers to adequately understand. The important discrimination is that our physical heart is not our Spiritual Heart. The physical heart keeps our physical body alive and vibrant; the other 'heart' is the Spiritual Heart, and many people have erroneously concluded that the Spiritual Heart is where the physical heart is. That is only partially correct. The only aspect of each and every one of us is that our souls are the only part of ourselves that is real. As it says in The Holy Bible, 'from dust to dust', and our soul will remember each lifetime as a memory and an illusion, and more often than not, soul growth and learning. Our Spiritual Hearts exist equally in all aspects of our souls and are totally indestructible and incorruptible. The proof of this is that our souls feel as clean and fresh as a new born baby when we truly forgive. However, many people get confused about that point since the physical heart can feel hurt and morally lost. People tend to erroneously conclude our Spiritual Heart is in the physical heart because that is where new oxygen with blood is pumped, and since it is a primary source of life for our body, we seem to generally feel more from our physical heart than from any other organ. So, the heart with the Infinity sign inside it is simply meant to illustrate that there is no limit to one's Spiritual Heart. And I believe that as we become more evolved, that we will become better in accessing the Spiritual Heart as we consciously work at using that incredible resource.

When I refer to The Holy Spirit, I will use He or Him rather than He/She or Him/Her in this book. I am very aware that The Holy Spirit is not partial to male or female gender, and that The Holy Spirit loves all people equally, i.e. with unlimited Love. This just happens to be a long-standing standard that most people understand and have no problem with. I mean absolutely no offense toward and no prejudice whatsoever against women. The presence of women and their wondrous ability to share love in this world will always be priceless and cherished in my mind and heart.

I believe some information about the name I have chosen for my publishing company (Winners Unlimited Publishing Company) would be important to mention. I believe all of us are destined to win at some point in time because of who our Creator is, even though many of us often seem to temporarily lose in our imperfect physical mortal bodies. So I am very much into a 'win-win' philosophy of life. Since we are forever connected to each other via our Creator, I strongly believe and know that if a person chooses to 'win' at the financial, physical, emotional, etc. expense of other people, then it is not a real win, and will come back as karma (what goes around comes around). And this is an excellent methodology to sufficiently motivate one to adjust and correct one's moral compass, for The Holy Spirit knows when your intent is pure, and when it is not pure. It is only when one learns to win in the way of The Golden Rule (do unto others as you would have them do unto you) will one's soul be pure enough in the consciousness of unconditional love and unlimited faith to enter The Kingdom of Heaven, which is not a physical location, but is a state of healed mind and spirit, and can be so with or without a physical body. This is something all those who are totally committed to do, will do at some point in time; some will take longer than others to accomplish this, depending on how much karma one has to learn the ways of unconditional love from.

And finally, I must make a legal disclaimer statement; that I cannot guarantee any healing or self-improvement for any person who reads this book. The reason is that a person's personal growth and spiritual progress is a choice each individual must make for himself/herself. I can only make choices for myself; I cannot make any meaningful choices for another person, for that is the gift that our Creator gave to each person, i.e. the power of choice. And the individual's personal growth and progress is dependent on the individual's intensity and depth of personal values and commitment. Therein lies each individual's amazing and abundant power. Another factor that could inhibit healing or self-improvement is misinterpretation of an important point because of misunderstanding of a word, sentence, stanza, or paragraph, for if the reader is not understanding the point clearly, that will likely cause misinterpretation. Physical dictionaries and online dictionaries are available to be certain of the meaning of a word, so please refer to one if you experience anything other than a positive response. I want to make it clear that this entire book is very pure in the intent to mentally and spiritually uplift and help as many people as possible (as guided by The Holy Spirit), and any interpretation contrary to that is absolutely in error, and should be corrected if one is to get the real benefits of this book. On the very positive side, the learning available in this book can give you the guidance toward the best path I know of for a fulfilling, peaceful, and happy life. However, although it is possible to attain spiritual mastery, it is important to know it may take several lifetimes to get to the level of Jesus Christ. But, over time I believe that we can and will attain his level of self-mastery in our own unique individualized way. Go forward with Faith and Love.

Table Of Contents

TITLE	PAGE
The Counterfeit Heart	12
Stubbornness	13
Veils Of Ignorance	14
The Open Soul	16
Take Time To Know Yourself	17
Close Ain't Enough	18
Know Thy Real Self	20
Will You Choose Truth?	21
True Winning	22
True Freedom	23
True Willingness	24
True Success	25
Logic of Success	26
Reinterpretation	28
What's Most Important	29
Fear Not Fear	30
Enlightened Intention	31
Expanding Inward	32
Personal Truth	33
Growing	34
Survival	35
Moral Intention	36
Personal Responsibility	37
Release The Beast	38
Past Reflections	40
The Rest Of Your Life	41
Authority, Power, And Integrity	42
Charisma	44
The Symphony Of Life	45
A Foot In Heaven	46
The Greatest Treasure	47
The Way Back	48
The Healing Feeling	49
The Invisible Lock	50
The Gratitude Attitude	51
Blue Skies Within You	52
A Clearer Mirror	53
Forgiveness, The Path To Inner Freedom	54
The Happy Moment	55
The Mansion Of Humanity	56
The Rebirth Of Dreams	57

TITLE	PAGE
A Taste Of Infinity	58
Excellence	59
New Horizons	60
Values	62
Is This The Way You Want It To Be?	63
Make It An Advantage	64
Guide Me	65
The Nature Of True Power	66
Stronger Longer	67
Praying, Knowing, & Destiny	68
True Strength	69
Inevitability	70
I Am You And You Are Me	71
Unlimited Communication	73
Unlimited Giant	74
True Greatness	75
Our True Father	76
Real Love	77
Vision	79
Ripples Into Eternity	81
Spiritual Transformation	83
What Will The Future Be Like?	84
Recommended Reading	88

The Counterfeit Heart

If your physical heart
Knows not your Spiritual Heart

Perception of the false
Seems more real than the true

And humanity suffers the loss
Affecting others, but mostly you

A counterfeit heart
Is known to start

When a child learns the best survival strategies
To best-as-possible prevent life's tragedies

Forced to learn that which is untrue
Imprinting the child's mind with an off-colored hue

So the child grows up with unconscious primal terror
Not really understanding the influential inner error

When will you finally come face-to-face
With the blocks to your innermost sacred place?

When will you choose to find
The Real Spiritual Heart inside?

Instead of the game that causes the greatest loss
The misguiding line on the game board of life

The counterfeit heart often chooses to cross
Producing a spiritually unfulfilling plight

The lost and misguided heart
Manufactures manipulative emotions

That cause illusions to start
Along with the accompanying commotions

The deep inner self never seems to be gratified
Always wanting more, and is rarely satisfied

When will you choose to transform that which is counterfeit within
So a peaceful and joyous heart can truly begin?

Stubbornness

So, how's your life really going?
What kind of seed are you sowing?

What can we expect of you
When given love or fear to do?

If love and fear is all there is
Which would be first on your list?

Any hostile thought from yourself
Will be returned above all else

Unless cathartic release is your pure intention
Only then will you experience ascension

Does the path you're on
Lead to Heaven?

You can choose that, you know
Isn't that where you want to go?

Why choose a different path
When it creates inner wrath?

Peace is ours to keep
Why not make the leap?

For when you've released all of your fears
Comes a joyous heart in upcoming years

For all eternity
The perfect unity

Knowing no limit or lack
And no motive for attack

What stubbornness would have you choose
A direction in which you would temporarily lose

That which brings the greatest treasure
And perfect peace and pleasure?

Veils of Ignorance

Let's choose deliverance
From our ignorance

Ignorance results from holding an invisible veil over your mind
Hiding your Ultimate Truths, making them difficult to find

What do you really know about True Reality?
Do you honestly know your life mission and Infinity?

Emotional scars create barriers and blocks
Our inner freedom caged with imperceptible locks

The ruts of life created by a sense of lack
Continue to bring an unhappy past back

To ignore that we all love each other
Is to hide The Truth from self and brother

Are we really enemies or friends?
"Love all people" makes most sense

How can we support each other with defenses up?
Will you offer a handshake, or emotionally erupt?

Why should our countries be so separated?
Wouldn't unity and peace make us truly elated?

Let's not ignore the priorities of our existence
Why don't we share Love instead of resistance?

There's really no excuse for ignoring your true nature
Our lives should be filled with Love and rapture

A choice to ignore personal growth and your potential
Will delay mankind's attainment of the desired level

Learn how to know what is real within
And strengthen our power to win

The Inner Self has the kindness and wisdom
To reveal the experience of The Kingdom

To ignore Truth, the most precious jewel
Is the most certain sign of a fool

We're not required to remain where we are
We can surpass limitation by far

Truth takes time for learning
Best hurry - time's burning!

If this isn't enough to get you going
Your resistance will make it tough on your growing

To ignore the importance of this message
Will only add to the present damage

Ignorance of The Truths of The Universe
Can only serve to make things worse

So let's work together to find the key
And that way we can all be free

The Open Soul

As I open my heart and mind in peace
I create the conditions for release and increase

I now choose to know The Truth more
Than I ever did before

All that is past is gone
I'm ready to move on

To create a new destiny
A more rewarding reality

I ask to be completely healed
I want life's best deal

Inflexibility no longer a part of me
So I can truly see

New exciting possibilities
That my desire transforms to probabilities

And my faith can see as real
Knowing I can is how I feel

Isn't there only one truly precious goal?
To be found only by the open soul

The Kingdom of Heaven within
Beckons and calls again and again

Take Time To Know Yourself

When you really want to know The Truths of The Universe
You'll find you need to seek within first

Only when you make that unlimited connection with our Creator
Will you find you love yourself and your brother

The battles and conflicts in the outer realm
Result from the battles and conflicts within

The hurt and anger you wish to do to other beings
Is simply a mirror of what you're internally seeing

Can you truly profit by striking others back?
The loss to yourself supports your belief in lack

Suppressed emotions will always return
To affect your life until you learn

To really know your own mind
Instead of drifting and blind

Knowing that you can play your part
In any role you choose to play

And touch others' blinded hearts
So they too can know everything's okay

Knowing trust and understanding within
To be drawn from again and again

Close Ain't Enough

As I look at the maze of my mind
What surfaces to consciousness is what I find

Each feeling and thought intangible and fleeting
Coming in, dashing out, and sometimes meeting

Agreeing with or opposing each other
Stretching desire to understand further and further

And sometimes when I feel deeply enough
I can see more clearly and rise above

I glimpse at the divine current of life
And see the insanity of strife

This divine inner force is the greatest treasure
And has let me know Love without measure

The beauty within you is lavish and abundant
A Light within that knows no limit

If you don't seek it, you surely are unaware
For eternity, it'll always be there

This inner freedom supplies your every need
And frees you from all destructive seeds

A foundation of Truth and Honesty with self
Will open the channels for happiness and health

And what can bring greater richness
To enjoy life and all its fullness?

The barriers created by intense hurt and pain
Causes the bitterness and hate to remain

So we try and try to forget the painful experiences
And makes us constantly believe we need defenses

We believe we need to be protective
Not realizing our own perception is defective

If everyone protects by attack
Then everyone will be striking back

Our own inner conflicts make us perceive threat
Freedom or limitation - which foundation will you set?

It's not easy to release hurts from the past
Bitterness tries to hang on and last

And must be purged by emotional release
So that there is no barrier to inner peace

We have eternity to find Love within
But remember - close ain't enough to win!

Know Thy Real Self

More important than anything else
I am being true to myself

Now I have a holy instant
Now I have no judgment

Now I know there is no guilt or sin
Now I have wisdom and vision

Now I have no fear
My heart and soul is clear

Now I have forgiven all
Now I hear a mighty Call

Now I know which way is best
How could I again settle for less?

Will You Choose Truth?

Truth itself seems to be a paradox –
Is nothing, yet everything
So unfilled and vacuous, yet so full and creative
So simple and brief, yet so infinite and unlimited
So straight and narrow, yet totally expansive and covering everything
So absolute and definite, yet so loving and freeing
So disciplinary, yet so undemanding
So heavy, yet so light
So present, yet so quiet
So full of power, yet so gentle
So fleeting, yet so lasting
So encouraging and helpful, yet so fought and ignored
So secret, yet so available
So confusing, yet so revealing

Truth says we're perfect as we are, yet lets us know when we need to correct our errors. Truth reveals what is real and what is illusion. Will you allow Truth to enter your life to dismantle your illusions and restore your sanity? The paradoxes of Truth will create confusion, mixed emotions, and temporary impasses until you are ready to 'see The Light'.

If you're not open to The Truth of your being and your unlimited nature, then you are free to go on fooling and cheating yourself. Ignorance of Truth is 'Hell' - to live Truth is the path to Heaven. When you want Truth, then allow yourself to experience your confusion, so that you will shed Light and Understanding on its unreality, thus creating a condition whereby the highest and most beautiful experience of The Kingdom of Heaven can be joyously realized from within for as long as you want.

True Winning

The Truth, more than facts
It goes beyond your 'act'

To tune out the will of Infinite Mind
Makes Truth seem hard to find

The ever-present cure
Your spiritual nature

Knowing only satisfaction
Instead of frustration

Anything done without Love
Obscures The Light from above

And all darkness within
Creates a sad illusion

Will your destiny be a rut,
With intent to say, "Yes, but ..."?

And then play victim with "Why me?"
When, in Truth, you really are free

Since now is all there is
Each delay is joy you missed

Will you set aside
Your worldly pride?

When will you start
To really open your heart

To that inner Voice
In which you rejoice?

Unhitch yourself from limitation
And know the joy of creation

Perfect Love is purity of thought and heart
This real treasure never departs

Abundance where it really matters
All is gone that tears and tatters

When will you choose your real beginning
And know the precious joy of true winning?

True Freedom

When our worldly senses can't detect
The higher laws of cause and effect

When we can't see what lies
Beyond our physical eyes

Suggests a blockage in the mind
Seeming to limit and bind

The illusion of struggle and fear
Need no longer be here

When your circumstances seem unrelated
To what you've consciously directed

A closer look at what you really feel
Will uplift the pretense and reveal

The pain you would keep unconscious
That which inhibits love and trust

When your inner alter of thought and feeling
No longer needs any healing

You will then know true freedom
And no more sense of limitation

The Truth has always been there
For you to have and share

A joy so great and powerful
Endless - exquisitely beautiful

For that which is beatific
Converges with the scientific

Limited only by imagination
Unleashing our power of creation

Knowing that our true nature
Is the state of rapture

The soul in its pure and free state
Is truly our destined fate

True Willingness

In all The Universe, what works best?
That withstands every test?

The universal law of return
How long 'til you learn?

Positive creates more positive
Negative creates more negative

If a defenseless child receives too much pain
Negative emotions will try to reign

Negativity not purified by The Light
Makes distortion from Truth seem right

Leading us into mental prison
Forgetting our precious power of vision

Perceiving ourselves to be little
Thoughts conflict in the middle

Illusion seeming more real than Reality
Having chosen limitation over Love's vitality

All the while feeling a greater force within
Knowing that we are here to win

A trust within the core of your being
No matter what your eyes are seeing

A knowingness that is really real
Without a doubt is how you feel

To know that your destiny is best sown
When you have made our Creator's will your own

Never again the illusion of fear
The cost to peace is too dear

True forgiveness will set you free
True willingness is the master key

Which can take only an instant
Or as long as you're resistant

True Success

What is success to you?
That which is deep and true?

What level do you wish to attain?
Is it one that will always remain?

What can be taken away
Can change your life some day

What of money and worldly power?
Like making bread without flour

And what of romance?
As elusive as chance

And what of friendship and being sociable?
With ego, is changing and negotiable

There's nothing wrong with attaining the above
The question is, do they include Real Love?

Have the goals you've reached
Returned genuine peace?

Success in only worldly terms
Causes the heart to burn

Wisely creating dissatisfaction
And promoting inner action

Teaching you the nature of true success -
Peace, inner freedom, joy, and happiness

Logic of Success

If one's feelings are suppressed, resistance to releasing pain and trauma from the past keeps one's awareness of the mind and heart stuck, and not open to important information from the subconscious and intuition.
If one's feelings are suppressed, releasing pain and trauma from the past clears a path, and opens one's awareness of the mind and heart to the unlimited power and clarity of the subconscious and intuition.

You will be at a creative problem-solving disadvantage when you are not in tune with or not listening to your subconscious and intuition.
You will be at a creative problem-solving advantage when you are in tune with and listening to your subconscious and intuition.

You can't truly succeed when you're unwilling to correct what doesn't truly work.
You can truly succeed when you're willing to let go of doing old patterns that don't work, and choose to seek for, find, and do what truly works.

You will not likely solve a problem until you've become aware of it enough to accurately define it.
You will likely solve a problem when you've become aware of it enough to accurately define it.

You will not like problems when you perceive them as burdens to weigh you down.
You will welcome problems when you see them as opportunities, bearing gifts and rewards to your soul.

You will not likely create motivation to solve a problem or complete a task if you don't truly value the solution enough.
You will likely create motivation to solve a problem or complete a task if you truly value the solution enough.

You won't believe you can achieve a specific result when "I can't" is stronger than "I can".
You will believe you can achieve a specific result when "I can" is stronger than "I can't".

"I can't" will remain stronger than "I can" as long as motivation is insufficient to overcome the obstacles.
"I can" is stronger than "I can't" when motivation is sufficient to overcome the obstacles.

You won't likely visualize a desired result when you aren't in tune with or not listening to your subconscious and intuition; i.e. you will likely not 'see' a complete picture of what you want in your mind.
You will likely visualize a desired result when you when you are in tune with and listening to your subconscious and intuition; i.e. you will likely 'see' a complete picture of what you want in your mind.

You are unlikely to begin doing the steps to a desired result when you don't adequately visualize it.
You are likely to begin doing the steps to a desired result when you adequately visualize it.

You won't be able to create truly fulfilling and rewarding results if you would intend to truly hurt others or yourself.
You will be able to create truly fulfilling and rewarding results if you would intend to truly love and support others and yourself.

You can choose to make unwise choices that cause you to fail, and find no real meaning or joy for your life, or
You can choose to learn how to make wise choices that cause you to succeed, and find real meaning and joy for your life.

You can choose to see yourself as defeated, unworthy, and a failure if you are unwilling to learn from your failures.
You can learn to be successful and find real meaning and joy in your life by using your failures as feedback to learn from.

You can choose not to commit yourself to your own success, and as a result, not accomplish what you're here for, and experience very limited or no fulfillment or joy.
You can choose to commit yourself to your own success, and as a result, accomplish what you're here for, and experience considerable fulfillment and joy.

Which path do you choose'?
The final outcome will be the result of what you have chosen.

Reinterpretation

That which is first seen and felt
Only begins mental ice to melt

The first perception like blinders on a horse
No expansive vision to The Source

Only when knowledge and awareness is sought
Is the experience felt in the heart

Only when intense repetition is absorbed within
Will the true learning really begin

Familiarities discarded for the higher level
Seeking Truth as if pounding on a bevel

Knowing that you will break through
The final thrust - last one for you

No longer perceiving illusion
Last time to experience confusion

Interpreting only True Reality
Perfect Love in totality

Remembering what you already knew
Is what we all, in time, will joyfully do

What's Most Important?

Mathematics is the perfection of the science of quantity. Wisdom is the perfection of the science of quality. All things in the universe are made of quality and quantity, thereby composing the nature of that component. Nature, the interrelationship of quality (wisdom) and quantity (mathematics), is the infinite energy of Love and The Universe. And this, in turn, is what creates the most incredible miracle of all time - Life! Love, and only Love and Its positive energy, is what supports life. That's why Love is and always will be the most important thing in The Universe and in all eternity.

Fear Not Fear

Fear that is suppressed and held in the unconscious is far more destructive than fear that you have consciously acknowledged, for when you are aware of a fear, you have empowered yourself to undo it. When you are not aware of a fear that is creating havoc in your life, you have no power to correct it. How can you correct an error until you have acknowledged that there is something within you that is creating limitation and/or destruction in your life? Will you choose to wait until a fear's destructive effects 'knock you across the head' through your experience of life to get your attention? And will you choose to use 'getting knocked across the head' through your experience of life as a grand opportunity to correct your errors of mind, or will you play victim and wallow in needless suffering and misery? When you resist your fears they persist and maintain their power over you.

Look within; correct the errors; forgive by experiencing and letting go of the past. Heal yourself for all eternity and be an unlimited, loving, positive, constructive, and powerful person.

Enlightened Intention

A mind can be strong
At either right or wrong

When you're believing what is wrong is right
The Truth is obscured from your sight

To ignore the way things really are
Will surely keep you in the dark

Your life will surely be amiss
While you practice unforgiveness

The Truth always crystal clear
Listen within and you will hear

Then you will know
Fear is false and Love will grow

For Love is without limit
And freedom comes with it

Forgiveness of the illusory past
Is where we will end at last

How mighty the experience of ascension! ...
Natural result of the enlightened intention

Expanding Inward

In my quest to be free
I see it happens inside of me

As I press gently inward
The mental barriers seem absurd

Feelings and thoughts which I had been unaware
Had nevertheless always been there

I discovered that my defensiveness
Had been costing me my aliveness

And I thought that the defensiveness was real
Not knowing the true reality my mind would reveal

I could only see glimpses of Light and understanding
My mind desperately wanted some expanding

I felt confused when Truth and illusion met
And temporarily experienced regret

The more intense, the greater the growth
Hell and Heaven - you'll experience both

Would you rather stay where you are?
Or move on to a brighter star?

Expanding inwardly -
Accurately realized outwardly

If you want more out of life
Stop hiding the inner strife

Acceptance of where you're really at
Allows peace and healing to enter that

There are no real limits - we are divine
Look within, and at a perfect time you'll cross the line

Personal Truth

From the inner
To the outer

Exists the illusion
Of confusion

Would you prefer manifestation
Or frustration?

What seems to be
The key for me

Is to look at the effects
Which can appear to be defects

Once you know the cause
You can see the laws

Which can bind or tease you
Or which can free and please you

Growing

As yesterday's problems are washed away
I begin to really enjoy today

Worldly problems become a laughing matter
Instead of griefs which would tear and tatter

You too can learn to look at life's ups and downs
Simply as illusions, which appear as valleys and mounds

Survival

Will you choose your higher nature -
That which is free and pure?

Or remain in the prison of survival -
And tolerate the poison of evil?

Money, power, winning, losing, competition -
What wisdom accompanies these motivations?

What is true prosperity and its treasures?
What is closest to Heaven and Its pleasures?

"In God we trust" has become "In money we trust"
And "being in love" has become "being in lust"

Has this gotten us real happiness and freedom?
On which foundation are we building our kingdom?

Lifestyle and the sense of security can be the ultimate thieves
If we sell out our inner freedom for temporary glories

Are you working for the buck instead of what you enjoy?
Are you willing to go for what brings the greatest joy?

Upside-down thinking makes us feel a sense of lack
"Give and receive" becomes "obligate and take"

"As ye believe, so shall it be" says it all
Choose real abundance and some old beliefs must fall

The Truth of abundance cancels greed and promotes sharing
And lets us see the real treasure of caring

Survival implies a belief in mortality
How could that possibly be True Reality?

The belief in the struggle to survive is all that makes it so
Will you discard this belief and really start to grow?

The chains of survival will dissolve with mankind's evolution
Will you join to win for peace in this final revolution?

Moral Intention

Thought which molds belief
Creates the forms you see

Our essence of consciousness
Producing our uniqueness

You as a component of The Universe
Your choice - for better or worse

Which energy predominates?
For Love, or for hate?

Purification or limitation
Salvation or damnation

Personal Responsibility

As I reveal the 'secret' of inner freedom to you
I sincerely want you to know it too

All that negative stuff you're getting
Is not worth the worry and fretting

What's most important -
The solution, or another negative result?

All confusion comes from inner conflict
Ambivalence - the first step to healing it

A weakening of the negative belief system
Begins the journey to the best solution

To acknowledge that you created your every experience
Brings you back to the most basic common sense

Our experience comes from our mind
What a simple solution to find

You get what you truly believe
How simple our eternal reprieve

Guilt and fear turn out to be
Negative beliefs which would keep you unfree

Forgive yourself for what you thought was true
And let go of the pretense you thought was you

Open the thought system of Love into your life
And you will know the joy and abundance of The Light

There's really nothing you can't do
When you become truly free within you

Release The Beast

Most of us try to hide
That we're a bit crazy inside

This is the beast of pain, fear and destructive emotions
Which always creates upsets and commotions

A part of your mind
Not willing to be kind

The pains of childhood can last you a lifetime
Not knowing true freedom - like a lock on your mind

Since pain is the nature of its inception
Its untruth will produce distortion

Envision a human body which Life did create
Purest of love energy - only first rate

When the foreign energy of pain entered
No longer with Pure Spirit were we centered

Distorting our perception
Experiencing imperfection

Throughout your defenseless body did the beastly energy spread
As with toxic potion had our veins been fed

Seeming to be part of your self
Seeming to have filled the cleft

Causing you to be needlessly limited
The negative energy makes us spiritually inhibited

As a caged animal rages for release
To hold on to your beast prevents inner peace

Socially unacceptable in its full intensity
So vicious games are played to vent the hostility

Fooling yourself to believe you're happy when you're really not
Never forgetting to play your role and all that rot

Spawning a need to believe when in error you're right
Which keeps you caught in your destructive plight

The beast within plays games of self-deception
Why believe a lie over The Truth of your perfection?

The beast can be ruthless in acts of oppression
To oppress yourself or others is proof of its transgression

Weakness, evil and sin
All come from the imaginary beast within

A seemingly awesome task to complete
This beast that we must release

The pain, fear and anger seem imbedded to your soul
In Truth, only an imprint - a removable shadow

Time to set the most meaningful goal
A total commitment of the soul

When the original trauma is fully experienced and released
You'll gain freedom from that part of your inner beast

Clearing the way for you to more clearly see things as they really are
Instead of missing the most rewarding target by far

Allow the beast the freedom to burn itself out
And with Spirit aglow will turn your life about

Know again your soul the way it came
Clear, loving and beautiful - forever the same

Do you want life's real feast?
Release the beast!

Past Reflections

How would you like the quality of your memories to be?
Are they rich with Love, or do they seem empty?

Do they have the flow of caring and friendship in your heart?
If not, when would you like that to start?

You can choose the foundation of your life
Will you choose brotherhood or strife?

Your relationship with your inner being
Determines the quality of the world you're seeing

Do you really and truly like the person you are?
Can you really believe you haven't an emotional scar?

Are your reflections at the level of happiness you really desire?
You can locate an inner beauty that will never tire

How are you at judging or compassion?
Which one is your preferred fashion?

The doors of Heaven can open from within
And all it takes is to decide to begin

It's more difficult to choose your own path than to follow like sheep
Will you commit to doing this, or do you think the climb's too steep?

Are you willing to accept and follow the evils of mankind?
Will courage to make a difference be your state of mind?

What will your reflections be?
What kind of memory?

The Rest of Your Life

How long from now to the date of your death?
When your lungs breathe their last breath

On that day
What will your soul say?

"Did I really want the roles I played?"
"Were they worth the efforts I made?"

"Did I really help or hurt humanity?"
"Did I approach my life with real character or with vanity?"

"Did I do what I really wanted to do?"
The only one that needs to know is you

Tomorrow always becoming today
So how do you want your life to play?

Listen to your divine Inner Voice
So you will always make the right choice

Patterns of the past can be hard to break
Are you willing to do what it takes?

Primal trauma affects your beliefs
Leading you into roles of self deceit

Let your heart-felt primal pains go
Through forgiveness you will know

What your best roles in life should be
To enjoy your chosen reality

What you really believe
Goes beyond what you perceive

Yet from your beliefs is your reality born
Including every object and form

Change your beliefs from deep within
And a new reality will begin

Knowing that all problems have a solution
Learning to tend to the cause more than the symptom

Resolving the problem at the level of mind
Makes the solution simple to find

How would you like the rest of your life to be?
As a 'victim' of circumstance, or on target to self-mastery?

Authority, Power, and Integrity

Who is better to give you authority than you
For all the things you do?

If not given the freedom to choose
Don't we all tragically lose?

How honest can you be,
More so with yourself than with me?

How many lies to yourself have you heard?
Isn't it important to keep your own word?

How can faith in yourself be solid and stay
If you don't believe what you think and say?

Are you wise in your choice of commitments?
What are the values that make most sense?

Seeds of integrity or the opposite are chosen
Each individual in each moment frozen

For you cannot undo the passing of time
The outcomes of each choice will be your sign

So you will know if you have chosen the right direction
Or gone the way of needless suffering

Do you have confidence in those without integrity?
Have you reached a high level of authenticity?

How do you affect other people's lives?
With Honor and Truth, or deception and lies?

Do you want others to feel your pain?
How would that give you any gain?

Only you know how you use your power and authority
Do people see you as a blessing or an atrocity?

Will you intentionally or blindly kill other's dreams?
Or choose mutual benefit via the opposite extreme?

If you kill other's dreams by not doing what you said you would
You harm yourself far more than you ever thought you could

Integrity's highest rewards will come to those
Whose hearts are truly loving and not closed

Can faith within yourself flourish
If your integrity is not nourished?

For trust is the vital lifeline for the Spirit within the heart
That ignites The Cosmic Fire that never falls short

Integrity is an inner choice
In which you are the only voice

To integrate mind, body, and soul
Is to be together and whole

Integrity is easily accomplished
When one has chosen forgiveness

Choose to gain wisdom from your experiences
For your choices make big differences

In those whose lives you touch
Do you care very little or very much?

Charisma

Answer honestly, who are you?
Another monkey in society's zoo?

Or another robot in a mechanical world?
The structure around which your personality has curled?

Do you tire of the commonplace?
The inner feelings are all you have to face

When did you last know your Real Inner Self?
When will you take your heart and gut off the shelf?

'Cause if you can't do that, you're only half-alive
And in that state of mind, it's harder to strive

So, if you want the aura of Life within you to glow
Get real with yourself and let charisma flow!

The Symphony of Life

If you weren't sure that your soul
Was a unique part of The Whole,

Would you try to be the conductor?
Perhaps a would-be dictator?

In a world of others doing the same
Whose will would reign?

The terrible racket of conflict and war
Is the loudest sound produced so far

If we all were in tune with The Infinite Mind
Then blessed harmony we would always find

And we would know the joyful melody of peace
A constant crescendo of all humanity's increase

With a triumphant new beginning
The synchronized chords of real winning

And when all the composing and arranging is through
The symphony of life can't be played without you

And you, and all souls around you will know
If you are out of tune, or enriching the flow

A Foot in Heaven

Are you cognizant
That people are resistant

To the open invitation
Of our inheritance of Heaven?

The transition period
Is often feared

Yet when both feet are sinking into the unhappiness of the world
And all your best efforts for happiness somehow become snarled

One must begin seeking for the best solution
That which offers an indestructible and eternal foundation

Putting one foot lightly on this new ground
Slowly adding more weight to check if it's sound

Finding its laws are different from the way of Earth
That you are far more than you thought you were

An attraction which you can't ignore
Pulls you into it more and more

To live in this world, and yet another
Seems to complicate life further

To see much more than meets the eyes
Makes one ask, "Am I foolish or wise?"

Others may scoff and judge you
For what you're strongly devoted to

A Master with a definite, yet invisible presence
A cause for which there seems to lack evidence

Yet The Light of Love is clearly recognized
As that which is most highly prized

And this highest experience can begin to happen
When you trust enough to put a foot in Heaven

The Greatest Treasure

Belief in the physical
Seems logical and practical

And the belief in time and space
Is seldom a state of grace

A harsh environment of limitation
The all-too-perfect demonstration

We'll all know it's true,
That we are eternally you

And you are eternally us
For that's the basis of trust

As we realize The Truth of our Creator
Bound by Perfect Love forever

The illusion of conflict dissipating
Peace glowing and radiating

The warmth of The Perfect Light
Makes all things right

Self-made prisons are such a waste
Even those approved in 'good taste'

Fear always blocks the mind
Of the beauty we're destined to find

Why would you choose rough stones
When the greatest treasure is your own?

For behind our distorted perception
Is The Truth of our perfection

Only you hold the inner key
To your True Reality

The Light or self-defeat,
Which treasure will you seek?

The Way Back

How lonely I've been
With people all around

My heart seemed untouchable
I felt unlovable

The wall of hurt blocking reality
Not hearing the Voice of Infinity

Bursting after the freedom of love
The only thing the heart knows of

To forgive does not mean forget
View everything without regret

All this useless suffering
That many are experiencing

The past is no longer here
To think so creates fear

The past binds you only if you let it
Why act out an old skit?

Our Father in Heaven is waiting
Within you - anticipating

The freedom of your heart
When will you let it start?

The Healing Feeling

An experience far beyond words
Makes talk seem absurd

A remembrance of who you really are
A Magnificence brighter than the brightest star

Undermining all belief in limitation
No longer valuing less rewarding temptations

Seeing yourself as much more than physical form
The Real You can never be harmed

A purpose higher than you ever thought of before
Arises from your inner being, your innermost core

A purpose of peace and mutual support
The highest rewards of harmony and rapport

To dissolve all illusions of conflict
Weakens evil's destructive grip

To bring us all the love and joy we deserve
A destiny for which our hearts truly yearn

Choose to let go of all unforgiveness and hatred
And you will know what is truly sacred

Once discovering only Pure Love within
A beautiful reality for you will begin

Experiencing oneness with all that ever was, is, or will be
Is to remember that we were created to be free

The 'secrets' of true freedom worth revealing
When will you enjoy the healing feeling?

For all humanity
For all eternity

The Invisible Lock

The hardest and easiest door to get through
Can be chosen only by you

The key seems nowhere around
You wonder, "How is it found?"

The best answer seems to be
"When will you choose to see?"

When your inner vision is blocked
You have chosen the invisible lock

Held by unreleased resentment and pain
To irritate the inner you again and again

Unexamined beliefs are given the power
To control your life every hour

Until The Light of Understanding is selected
To see what needs to be corrected

Forgive yourself for blocking your inner sight
Through the unlimited love of The Light

Miracles - the harvest of a forgiven past
A state of mind that can always last

Loving yourself and others too
Is best for all of you

It's really simple, you see
The invisible lock has an invisible key!

The Gratitude Attitude

When one feels sad, angry, frustrated, or hateful
This tends to make one feel ungrateful

Seems to be all too common on this planet
Leading one to conclude that this is the world's limit

Yet when you release the negative thoughts and feelings
You can blow out the mental ceilings

Since we are all children of The Unlimited Mind
Our connection to our Creator is all we need find

How could we not have a grateful heart
When we've been given everything from the start?

The grateful heart is the unfailing magnet
That attracts the unlimited power of The Holy Spirit

And once His miraculous will has begun
You will see how much you've won

Ascending to a much higher latitude
When you choose the gratitude attitude

Blue Skies Within You

Would you block the blue skies within you?
Must life be colored with a dark hue?

The colors of your inner being
Create the world you're seeing

Would you allow dark clouds to cover your inner vision?
When will you allow the full spectrum of your true mission

To illuminate your consciousness
With the rainbow of forgiveness?

So that you may radiate The Light
With unlimited strength and might

When will you allow the texture of your soul
To be again made clear and whole?

When will you allow the canvas of your destiny
To be divinely stroked by the Hand of Infinity?

A Clearer Mirror

What thoughts project from your mind and soul?
Are your acts warm, or vengeful and cold?

What do you actually hold dear?
Light and Love, or darkness and fear?

How much Light do you allow
To shine through you now?

Inner barriers add to the darkness and pain
Preventing The Light that would make you sane

Perception determines choice
Creating your life's course

Is the quality of your perception
Distorted by fear and self-deception?

Or alive with an inner reflection
Of Love's eternal perfection?

The way you see your brothers
Is how you see yourself in others

Is the image someone you really like?
Is the glow from within dark or bright?

It's really no secret -
What you give is what you get

When no barriers remain
On the inner plane

Light will shine through
To reveal the Real You

And see in your brothers' eyes
The Truth that always satisfies

So, which reflection of life would you prefer -
The present image, or a clearer mirror?

Forgiveness, The Path To Inner Freedom

Forgiveness seems to involve four stages. First, a realization that there is an inner barrier which is restricting your life force; an irritation locked in unconsciousness causing a sour or bitter attitude - never feeling fully satisfied or happy, sometimes fooling yourself into thinking you like the circumstances in your life, when deep inside you really feel unhappy.

Second, a realization that projection of your hurt and anger toward people and circumstances in the outer world is inappropriate and is creating additional upheaval and conflict in your life, thereby causing you to struggle more to make it. At this stage you are trying to forgive those outside yourself, but never are fully able to do it, and you may often wonder why.

Third, a realization and experience that your thoughts and beliefs are all-powerful and are attracting the people, situations, and circumstances in your life. At this stage you begin to realize that forgiveness of others is a step in the right direction, but does not yet attain the desired result. You see that you must forgive yourself for creating a reality (actually an illusion) divergent from joy and our Creator's will. In this stage you discover that it was not our Creator creating your misfortunes, but your own defiance of our Creator's perfect authority of Unconditional Love and Truth. You learn that you must forgive yourself for separating yourself from His infinite glory, and for believing you were entrapped in a mortal body and experiencing the illusion of fear. Trust comes when you allow Him to express His unlimited love and power through you, and to know that He communicates with you through your heart-felt feelings and pure desires.

Fourth, a realization and experience that you are invulnerable in the truest reality and can never really be hurt, thereby realizing that forgiveness is needed only where there is self-inflicted condemnation. An implication of this is that your hang-ups appear to come from childhood, but in Truth you chose your parents and created your childhood from an unhealed state of mind and heart in accordance with the karma you came into this lifetime with. Final forgiveness is to forgive yourself for not remembering that the only thing real about your life is your eternal Spiritual Self, and for creating a temporary and mortal physical body, living your life in that physical body, and believing as if it were real rather than the illusion that it is. At this stage your erroneous feelings and thoughts are corrected, then purified and spiritualized, and your life and creative forces are multiplied to create the natural state of miracle-mindedness, and the ability to be a catalyst to cause them to happen by the unlimited power of The Holy Spirit. Your awareness of the beauty of the cause and effect relationship of the universe is regained so that you are at cause in creating your destiny, rather than at the effect of your environment and playing victim. We are born to win. This is the road to peace, self-mastery and true freedom.

The Happy Moment

This moment starts
With true forgiveness in the heart

When the pains of the past
Are fully purged at last

Each moment will be anew
The past no longer limiting you

Discarding the false and accepting the true
Leads to knowing what you really want to do

And once knowing this
Nothing is amiss

And each moment is lived most fully
When you perceive all as holy

And in your oneness with all
Will not again think small

And you will radiate peace and love
What we all want more of

Real Love comes to the heart and mind
The true winner who is gentle and kind

Who has found that each passing minute
Has the happy moment in it

The Mansion of Humanity

Why perpetuate thoughts and actions
Which weaken humanity's foundation?

Why participate in corruption and dishonesty,
Or anything that weakens our dignity?

Must we add more scars
And worsen the way things are?

Our foundation is in need of repair
We play the games of fear and despair

What lurks behind
The entrance to your mind?

Will you hurt your brother
Or support each other?

Has The Master Architect made a mistake,
Or has He made something really great?

We're all in The Master Plan
Choose Faith and lend a hand

The joy is in the doing
Let's set our goals and get moving

Purity of heart and intention
The ultimate ascension

The walls of resentment must fall
Replaced by true forgiveness for all

The return to our home of Love and sanity
Forever within The Mansion of Humanity

Definition: (from Webster's Dictionary)
Dignity - The quality or state of being worthy, honored or esteemed

The Rebirth of Dreams

Was there a dream that broke your heart and soul?
One that you really wanted, but somehow failed your goal?

Do you think it might do you in
If you tried and failed again?

Are you afraid you'll create more
Of what you did before?

Or would you apply a basic rule?
Use your failures as learning tools

Where would you be without dreams
To create a reality that shines and gleams?

Without dreams your soul is in poverty
Finding the illusion of darkness and scarcity

What do you want most of all?
What inside you has the truest call?

What would you choose to go toward
That would produce the highest reward?

Are you living the way you really want to live?
The pattern from failure to success - the vital shift

How long will you allow the pains of the past
To keep you from the joy that will forever last?

When pain and fear have been released
Confidence and Faith will increase

When will your new dreams unfold?
Will you choose Faith's abundant threshold?

For you can choose how high
You really want to fly

The dreamer reborn within
With new wisdom to win

Welcome the rebirth of dreams
And the inspiration each one brings

Behold! The seeds of new beginnings
Will one day reap the harvest of winning

A Taste of Infinity

Pain and fear block our infinite nature
Of that I am sure

Deep hurts of life try to remain
Like a festered sore to bring more pain

Our minds have total recall of the events
Which were painful enough to create a defense

So, we lost trust in the completeness of creation
And approached the true realities with hesitation

Without trust in the divine flow
We learned to manipulate and control

And we temporarily forgot our connection with The Infinite
And trusted only in the physical-survival level and its limits

Many fear change when change was previously painful
To not know our own strong and powerful Self is what's most sinful

To seek Truth is to 'squeeze' our emotional sores
And let the hurt flow through to open mental doors

Thus creating a mental space
Unveiling The Infinite for you to 'taste'

Once savoring your Infinite Light within
A banquet of nourishing values will begin

To go for peace and love all of the way
To create and share your joy and abundance every day

To know Truth is to be free
How else could it be?

Are you really happy with your present perception of reality?
No matter - you have infinity to find Infinity

In life, you create your own happy or unhappy story
Why wait a moment longer to taste Infinity and Its glory?

May your spiritual taste buds know Truth in full measure
And allow your life to become infinite pleasure

Excellence

Shoddy workmanship
A societal handicap

How often does mediocre work adversely affect you?
Do you do poor or mediocre work too?

Delivering low quality of work
Does not enrich one's pocketbook

Would you rather be a parasite to society
Or a strong supporter of humanity?

How can we truly enjoy our vocation
When talents and tasks have no relation?

Each of us has a unique consciousness
Why try to be like anyone else?

A unique creation should remain so
To move that way is to grow

Resolve to know the Real You
And discover what you can possibly do

There's at least one thing you can do really well
An inherent ability in which you excel

A skill in which you naturally specialize
Which the 'norm' might criticize

Know the quality of your talents
And discover your own excellence

The more you experience your Real Identity
The more you prosper and enrich all humanity

With the full range of talents we each have individually
Isn't it possible for talents and tasks to match equally?

A wide variety of worldly tasks need to be done
Each person can use their talents while having fun

All people's talents blending in synchronized harmony
Breaking the unfulfilling work monotony

All people feeling useful and fulfilling their life purpose
Their lives greatly enriched benefiting all of us

With survival needs met in an enjoyable way
Problems caused by poverty will simply drop away

Time to end the masquerade of unconsciousness
And participate in the era of unlimited awareness

If humanity is to survive and have a decent quality of life
Anything short of making positive changes is mass suicide

Commitment to excellence, the key to brotherhood
The Possible Society? Yes, we could!

When enough of us choose to soar to true excellence
We will dissolve all barriers and resistance

And will share abundance of peace and happiness
There to find we are truly limitless

New Horizons

Is your profession a heart-chosen role?
For then you have a commitment of the soul

Knowing the laws of the universe
Listening within and choosing them first

Profession - to profess unique knowledge
Serving your brothers - the first pledge

Always increasing the quality of you
So others will be lifted too

Resisting the temptations of prejudice and evil
Never allowing a fall to a lower level

Being a leader of Love and Light
Having the guts to stand for what's right

What new horizons will you create?
Choose wisely - for you will make your fate

Values

Without a doubt,
Have you figured your life out?

You may have flaunted
What you thought you wanted

And then you learned something more meaningful
Which brought conflicts by the handful

You question what values give a strong foundation
That will stand the changes of time and others' determination

What can you really believe in?
That will hold through thick and thin?

Is The Universe created in a haphazard way?
Or are there laws with infinite harmony?

Truth must have a uniformity
If not, simplicity would be lost with infinity

To choose Truth through your journey of life
Will always make results turn out right

What you value today may seem meaningless tomorrow
So flow with life and all its joy and sorrow

And what higher value than to love and share?
And let yourself know that you really care?

And once you've remembered Truth's pure essence
You'll shun the idea of pretense

Is This The Way You Want It To Be?

And what of the power of faith?
What must first predicate?

Isn't a forgiven heart needed first,
For attunement to The Universe?

Perfect communication with our Spirit of Light
Wisdom that always guides you right

A sensitivity that transcends pain
A vision beyond the physical brain

A hearing that listens to the quiet peace of the soul
An awareness that understands The Greater Whole

A spontaneity that knows no error
That surpasses being witty or clever

An Inborn ingeniousness within you
Accompanied by the inspiration to do

A Spirit, undying and without limit
That always shouts, "Go for it!!!"

Eternally there in you and me
Always asking, "Is this the way you want it to be?"

Make It An Advantage

Make it an advantage
That's the eternal message

The Truth of who we are
Heals the emotional scar

How can one be crucified
Who is pure Spirit inside?

Is pain really real?
It seems real to feel

Yet when the next moment is here
There is nothing left to fear

For once the past is gone
What good does it do to hold on?

Holding on to your pain
Can only make you insane

Unforgiveness without release
Is sure to cost you inner peace

When you choose to perceive Love
It affirms what you're made of

Wouldn't you be amused
If you knew that you could use

Every experience in the positive sense
Rather than to make you more tense?

You make it an advantage
When you choose Love's message

Guide Me

I heartily invite Your presence
Our only true Father in Heaven

Into the purest sanctuary
Of my heart and soul

Without Your wisdom and guidance
I stumble and fall in my path of life

I feel lost without the awareness of Your presence
With You there is abundance of all things

Guide me to an unshakable ground of being
Let my cup runneth over in the ocean of Your love

Guide me to the eternal oasis of Your joy
Let me know the boundless strength of Your peace

Guide me to Your mystical wisdom
Let me demonstrate Your kindness and gentleness

Guide me to Your true righteousness
Let me be a humble shining example

Guide me to true freedom
Let me skyrocket to Your sky of mind

Guide me to the oneness of The Universe
Let me see the big view

Guide me to Your miraculous will
Let me be Your channel of expression

Guide me to have faith in myself
Let me know You are always there

Guide me back to myself and my brothers
For that is where You reside

Guide me so I can lead others back to You
Let me so we all can win

Thank You Father
Amen

The Nature of True Power

What is true power and what is it like?

It is not power over others, although the ego would have you believe it is, and would try to tempt you into a power trip (the illusion of power).

It is mutual support and upliftment.

It is not a result of worldly wealth, politics, sex appeal, contrived manipulation, force (military, fighting technique, strategy, etc.) or any similarity, although the ego would tempt you to believe otherwise.

It is a natural outcome of a divine purpose whose directions and guidance come from the deepest part of one's soul, and is motivated by our oneness with The Universe and the greatest good and gain to all.

It does not lie in the separateness, exclusiveness and the one-upmanship of arrogance.

True power exists within all of us, and comes with the deep inner acceptance of your most rewarding and fulfilling roles in life; i.e. being true to yourself.

True power instills trust in all those who would share true power; it often evokes resentment and hostility from those whose consciousness is temporarily lost in the vanity of the ego and its illusion of power, because their entire thought system and its erroneous values are fully threatened in the mighty presence of the unlimited and true power of The Light of Real and Perfect Love.

Those who are committed to the illusion of worldly power fear being dominated and hurt because they unconsciously know how they would misuse their power if they were in charge, and thus would expect others in charge to be that way. In addition, change can be very painful, and they unconsciously know they will see the need for positive change around such inner beauty and awesome attractiveness of Real and Perfect Love.

The illusion of power creates problems because it lacks Real Love. True power creates solutions because Real Love for all humanity is its foundation. Which do you think would work best for all humanity? Which one do you choose to use?

Stronger Longer

What is truly weak
And what is truly strong?

What is truly right
And what is truly wrong?

If fear is hidden from the conscious self
Its struggle to stay hidden reigns above all else

Yet no matter how strong one appears to be
With fear, one believes in vulnerability

Undoing the negative belief of fear
Can be the only creator of inner strength

For what in your heart you hold dear
Will retard or advance you a great length

Only Love offers everything you want
Not fear, which would tease and taunt

Fear offers only lack and taking
Love offers only abundance and giving

So, if Love makes me very strong
For very long,

Then I would choose to be stronger longer
And strongest longest

And always choose Love as the motivating force
That always leads me right, of course

Praying, Knowing, & Destiny

Why aren't all prayers truly heard?
Why aren't all prayers really answered?

Is it possible for each individual's prayers to be granted?
Inevitable conflicts would lead many to be disenchanted

Since The Holy Spirit cares deeply for all souls
The prayers He grants must be for The Greater Whole

And this can only be known by the Ultimate Being of Wisdom
The clear awareness of what we need to return to The Kingdom

So, when praying, listen to that deepest inner Voice within
And first ask if your prayer is in harmony with The Divine Plan

One can only have faith that the prayer will come to pass
If the union with The Holy Spirit is steadfast

Knowing and Truth ring clear as the proverbial bell
And once truly 'hearing' this, your prayer will be granted as well

With your prayer in The Hands Of Infinity
You have helped the enhancement of Divine Destiny

And you will have done your vitally needed part
In this most important spiritual art

Enthusiastically knowing then
That you can do this again and again!

True Strength

The Spiritual Heart is not of the physical
Its nature is rather mystical

The gentle energies of the Spiritual Heart
Moves more than oceans could part

More powerful than stars exploding
Love's lightness infinitely bounding

For within the Spiritual Heart's core
Is the faith that brings you more

Unveiling the 'secrets' of the universe
Love energy - truly limitless

True strength comes naught
Unless there is purity of thought

You have an unlimited mind
You can thus heal and be kind

Heal the emotional blinds that distort your vision
And succeed at any loving mission

Will you justify false limitations,
Or let your heart go on vacation?

Learn all you can of Love
And all will come from within and above

And know that you are eternal joy
The world is simply our toy

Where you can come from a Mama
And experience a little drama

So, do you want to be limited
Or free and uninhibited?

Listen to your Spiritual Heart and true feelings
And you will begin your healing

Inevitability

Though we may conflict now
Things will brighten up somehow

Our participation
In the divine plan

Can only be perfect ...
True Reality beckons

Peace and harmony
An inevitability

When you allow peace into your heart
You see life a different way

Eager to support the brotherhood of man
As we acknowledge our Creator in each other

My heart thrills to see that day
Mutual support along the way

A most-valued common goal
Making diamonds of coal

Seeking and finding
The greatest treasure

How much time and misery
Before you accept the only inevitability?

I Am You And You Are Me

When you and I can see
That I am you and you are me

All barriers of fear will dissolve
And all unforgiveness will be resolved

For that which made me
Also made you

Within us all
Is a timeless Light

That prevails over all
And radiates Perfect Love

Throughout the universe
In every conceivable realm

In that sharing and unison of mind and heart
Will all bitterness and mistrust depart

Then differences will be seen as uniqueness
Rather than as a reason for separateness

The most exciting adventure of abundance for all
We but need listen to the mightiest call

Each one using the talents he enjoys most
Creating a reality of splendor for all of us

The boundless harvest of miracles is always there
For all who sincerely want to share

The unconditional love of our Father
For the remainder of forever

And this limitless joy begins to happen
When we truly choose The Kingdom of Heaven

Needless suffering, pain, and all that's insane
Or a joy soaring high above this plane

The feelings and thoughts you choose and hold are mine
It works vica-versa you'll find

Shall we belittle each other in deception, mistrust, and lies
Or see the wondrous enchantment in each other's eyes?

It matters to you as much as me
For we will know that we are free

When you and I can see
That I am you and you are me

Unlimited Communication

Do you gain gratification
From your communications?

Does your soul touch others with depth?
Or do you too often feel inept?

Have you noticed that a few are meaningful
While most others are superficial?

Why is compatibility limited to so few?
Inadequate numbers of committed people simply won't do

How can you accept distortions of authenticity in others
If you haven't cleaned out you own mental gutter?

The conflicts and self-hate within
Will cost you peace again and again

To the degree you resist intimacy and sharing
Will indicate how your own soul is faring

So, please make understanding your goal
When you peer inside another person's soul

Once you've learned where you think you're weak
The door to strength you'll no longer need to seek

Once opening the door to your own joy and peace
More abundance and joy will be on the increase

Unlocking the heart to unlimited possibilities not thought of before
Your love and creative capacity will soar and soar and soar!

If everyone shared Real Love and really communicated
All sense of hostility would be eradicated

Will you clear out your conflicts within
So you can communicate and really win?

Unlimited Giant

I see The Unlimited Giant in you
Do you see The Unlimited Giant in me?

Hate and fear belittles and deflates
Real Love expands beyond time and space

Love is the only reality that has no end
So it must be in all of us without guilt or sin

Once we all know who we really are
We'll see that we're all superstars

Each a vital part of The Whole
In the deepest part of our soul

Love is the only thing real between us
In eternity, how could there not be trust?

Let's end pain and suffering for all time
When we do, humanity can really climb

Beyond any form of destruction
Beyond scarcity and destitution

Your real intention has great influence
And that energy affects each instant

See how each person glows from within
As our faith in each other grows and ascends

As the world becomes a more loving place to live
We'll all gain strength to give

Will you see The Unlimited Giant in us
While we see The Unlimited Giant in you?

True Greatness

Let's be still and realize
Where true greatness lies

This person knows where to mentally go
The Real Inner Self allowed to flow

Knowing outer appearance is so deceiving
Yet can also be very revealing

The inner eye always projecting
On Love's eternal perfection

Having unlimited power
Yet benign as a flower

Not wishing power over another
Seeing all people as his brother

His values solid for the good of humanity
Leading his brothers back to health and sanity

His heart-felt beliefs are infinitely strong
His presence makes positive events come along

Where is this person?
Please make your presence certain

In reality he is here and present
We are simply waiting for your commitment

All are truly called to this greatness
To serve with the power of our uniqueness

You may not need to change your roles
Transform the quality of your goals

Your heart will furnish the full commitment of the soul
How else can we individually and collectively be whole?

Aren't we much better off and happier
When we share pure Love with each other?

The more people that make the conscious choice to commit
Will exponentially expand the prosperity of humanity without limit

We are Whole when we are One
Help our Creator's will to be done

Our True Father

Being God
I could create

Either something
Or nothing

If you were Me,
Which you are,

Ask yourself,
"What would I do? ...

Do nothing
Or enjoy Myself?

By watching My children
In their movie of life?"

So, I created The Divine Plan ...
Everything unites to perfection

I can only love
What I create

For I am Perfect Love
And know naught of judgment

I loved you so much
I gave you free will

And infinite powers of mind
To play with and learn

Knowing that you could and would
Limit and imprison yourself

But will always come back
To the freedom and warmth of My Light

And the total safety
Of My True Reality

Even if you don't believe in Me
I created you to be free

I am you
I am The Source

I love you
Always, of course!

Real Love

How often do you find
A real person - gentle and kind?

One who loves without condition
Or selfish ego intentions

One who values peace and brotherhood
A person who is truly good

One who lives The Golden Rule
Eyes that smile with Love for you

Can't we all be that way?
We can start today

How could multiple Creators
Create a perfectly consistent universe?

How could they possibly agree
On every little detail we see?

There can only be One
From which we've all begun

From our unconditional Love Source
His unlimited gift of the Life Force

Our connection of oneness with All
True vision perceives the mighty call

The only way for us to truly win
To value The Truth beyond illusion

That we're all indestructible
And totally, eternally loveable

Attack and defense
Only in necessity will make sense

Until we evolve beyond conflict and war
After which we will go very far

Until then, the good need to be strong
And use the best means to overcome wrong

Afterwards, attack and defense
Will make no sense

Unless we choose to invest
In an unreal premise

Eternally joined are we
How else could it be?

Will you choose to see and share
The Real Love that's always there?

This is the vital foundation of trust
That creates peace for all of us

Vision

How far can you see?
Is your mind really free?

Is your imagination
Free from limitation?

You can choose that
Or stay where you're at

Be not afraid to dream
Dwell not on how things seem

The world is constantly changing
A dynamic flow of rearranging

Claim your influence and power to sway
The way things are each day

Focus on your power to create
For your choice becomes your fate

Will you dream little and small
Or big and tall?

Will you expand your sight
All the way to The Light?

The dreamer often criticized and condemned
By those having fear within them

When you know a better way
Let not your vision stray

For what was not accepted by some before
May become sought after by more

If your vision has great value
Let no one mislead you

Should you somehow fail at first
Propel yourself forward, not reverse

The world suffers the cost
If your priceless dream is lost

Will you let your precious vision
Become your fulfilling mission?

For what you gain real joy from doing
Is a great treasure - growing ... accruing

How great will your vision be?
We'll see ... we'll see ...

Ripples Into Eternity

Mere catalysts are we
In the sea of eternity

For all around your cortex
Lies an all-powerful vortex

What energy are you feeding it?
What will you create this very minute?

Beliefs most often reside in your unconsciousness
Suppressed and buried from your conscious-awareness

Their power is awesome
Will you fight or heal them?

Would you deny your self-mastery?
Or be the captain of your destiny?

By surrendering to the flow of The Power within
Letting your feelings guide your life with Love again

What purpose for your voyage of life do you choose?
The trade winds to humanity's highest values?

Uncharted vessels often fall prey
To the doldrums of meaningless work or irreverent play

The shores of life are abounding
With downhearted derelicts resounding

Who never understood deeply enough
That their inner sea was rough

For they have drifted away from their harbor of Love and peace
Into a dense fog of pain, fear, and darkness

Then they became lost
At such an extreme cost

How could they trust themselves?
How could they trust anyone else?

Yet for the emotionally healthy and the cripples
Love creates gigantic ripples

Touching, bringing peace, and healing many
And in Its path, leaving a wake of harmony

For we clearly remember how acts of Love make us feel blessed
Yet pain, once released, is but a shadowy memory at best

Hurricanes of hate and bitter resentment
Turn calm with understanding and peaceful intent

Turning our attention
To The Truth of our creation

Each caring thought that goes out to others
Returns in positive unexpected ways via the ethers

Political, racial, religious and social differences
Will no longer make any sense

Away with the anchors of prejudice and limitation
Replaced by true equality and freedom

And once this inner mutiny is undone
Then our grandest dreams can be won

Mutual support abounding with abundance for all
Miracles happening with our slightest inner call

Time itself unveiled as a clever illusion
As we return to the eternal port of The Kingdom

And these possibilities all start with you and me
Each moment ... our ripples into eternity

Spiritual Transformation

How important is the peace and freedom of your soul?
Will this now be your most important goal?

If not, don't waste your time and effort for now
Wait until it becomes your top priority somehow

Unfulfilling events will likely temper your desire and motivation
That will lead you on the journey to spiritual transformation

Free will and total commitment are vital
For the greatest personal reward of all

Meditate, pray, do Yoga, fast, go to a good psychotherapist,
Get into Nature, do positive affirmations, and anything else that helps

To seek, find, discover, experience, and be your Real Inner Self
For this endeavor will be one of your most difficult tasks

But will be the most rewarding accomplishment
That will be realized by yourself and all of humanity

What Will The Future Be Like?

Some of you readers may think that I live in a delusion of fantasy, and that the concepts in this book are very unrealistic in this world. I'll quickly admit that it is more difficult for people to enjoy life in this world while there are so many delivering their ego-borne selfishness, cruelty, deceit, inconsiderateness, etc., but that makes it all the more important that we live and demonstrate unconditional love and caring by emulating The Holy Spirit, for that has a miraculous transforming effect on people as Jesus Christ demonstrated. This book is about True Reality, and is the desirable outcome that we as a civilization will eventually evolve to. Our technological evolvement has progressed beyond our motivation and willingness to listen to and follow the inner guidance of our Spiritual Heart. If enough of us pray with faith, we will not have a devastating nuclear war before getting to that point in our Spiritual Heart evolution. The Holy Spirit has revealed these Truths to me to communicate to all of humanity. Fortunately, His way is a much better reality than we have made up to this point.

Consciousness is a term used more often in the last few decades. Although it originally meant conscious-awareness, my observation is that it more and more means the totality of an individual's overall mentality, i.e. including conscious-awareness, the subconscious (easily retrievable to conscious-awareness), the unconscious (not easily retrievable to conscious-awareness), and the super-conscious (related to supernatural) aspects of the individual's mind. So it follows that mass consciousness is the mental sum or mental totality of all human beings. Mass consciousness and critical mass are the key concepts, which are very similar to the concept of the hundredth monkey. There is a popular and very important book called 'The Hundredth Monkey', and the main point of the book is that in several observations of monkeys, that when a monkey begins doing something notably new or different that is usually helpful to the monkey community, that as enough monkeys mimic that behavior and cause a critical mass of monkey consciousness in that monkey community, other monkey communities begin doing the same thing, even though they are sometimes hundreds of miles from each other (and in some cases on different islands), and have no way of observing the other far away monkey communities. And prior to this new behavior, none of them were doing this new behavior. This means that there is an unseen supernatural connection between all of the same genus of monkeys, and although they may not be aware of the connection, it nevertheless significantly affects their lives.

Since human beings are the dominate and most intelligent species on this planet, and since we are all divinely connected by our Creator, how could this hundredth monkey phenomenon not be affecting us as well? I'm certain it has been affecting us since human beings began living on Mother Earth, ever increasing as our consciousness evolves. We know, for example, that when inventors were working on a significant invention idea that there were others working on it as well. Alexander Graham Bell was not the only one working on communication over distances too great for normal talking, and the Wright brothers were not the only ones working on creating a vehicle that could transport people in the air. It is well known that some people are psychic, and can 'see' things clearly and accurately that most people aren't aware of, and many of them are quite accurate in enough detail to know that their statements are true. It follows that they are mentally connected to that higher power and our Universal Oneness. The true reality is that all of us human beings are connected to each other by our Creator, and thus we are unlimited, individually and as a six billion plus group. We cannot avoid being a part of this, and how it affects our lives, whether the effect is positive or negative, depending on the mental totality of mass consciousness at that particular time.

Throughout the history and evolution of humanity, since we are separate physical entities, there have always been individual struggles and accomplishment. However, one cannot help but notice that significantly much more is accomplished when people work together for a common cause or purpose. And now we have a huge and gigantically important cause that a significant and adequately large number of us need to work together on to effectively create a critical mass to prevent humanity from committing mass suicide, i.e. extinction of the human race. The way we do it is very important, and the way to win this 'war' is by enough people making an unlimited and total commitment to the growth of their consciousness to the internal attainment of faith in themselves. The 'symptoms' of True Faith are inner calmness, peace, grace, composure, emotional and mental self-mastery, and unconditional love; and it is something that must be real to be believable; i.e. no one can fake it for long and be truly believable. One individual with total faith (similar to Jesus) can possibly bring about that vital critical mass, but many people with enough faith can cause humanity to attain this all-important objective substantially more quickly, which I suspect will be vitally needed before long on a timely basis. These people can be of any age; even a child or a very old person can wield gigantic power with his/her faith. People with real faith usually are not harried or running around hurriedly in fear. And they are very spontaneously deliberate in their every move, naturally displaying the self-mastery of faith. Their faith naturally mobilizes our Creator's supernatural forces, and miracles are commonplace for such a person. Fortunately, we are all capable of this when we have completed the process of complete and true forgiveness.

The interesting phenomenon of Divine Intervention sometimes occurs, and when it does, it is amazing to all who are paying attention. Most often when Divine Intervention occurs, It often takes the form of some natural occurrence or disaster, and appears to be a result of natural Cause and Effect. The parting of the water for Moses and his people is the most famous example. Another good example is the rough weather during the D-Day landing in World War II. Although we had eliminated nearly all of the German fighter planes and German U-boats near that area in northwestern France, if the weather had been good, the Nazis would likely have had better intelligence on a landing of Allied troops. But they believed that General Eisenhower would not make a supposedly unwise decision of landing our invasion force in such bad weather. Had the Germans detected our invasion, their response would have likely been considerably more aggressive and destructive to the

Allies landing on the beaches in Normandy, and many more Allied soldiers would likely have been killed. I believe the bad weather was a Divine Intervention to prevent the world from being ruled by a ruthless dictator. A few more thousand German soldiers with machine guns, mortars, etc. in their virtually bomb-proof bunkers would likely have killed many thousands more Allied soldiers. Had that happened, we may not have had enough troops and equipment to overwhelm them, and the atomic bomb might have been dropped on them first (before Japan) to win the war, or the Germans might have had enough time to create the atomic bomb first and win the war (what a nightmare that would have been for the world!). The ramifications in terms of destiny are huge.

Divine Intervention is one big factor we have no control over, and may one day kill or save many of us. However, we are all going to die eventually; it's simply a matter of when and how. The most important thing to remember is that if it is not your time to die, nothing can make it happen, and when it is your time to die, nothing can stop it from happening. Death is nothing to fear because it completes your life, and puts you back into our Creator's 'hands' of Love to communicate the most unconditional and wondrous love He has for all of His children. A byproduct of one who is not afraid of death is that he/she will cherish life all the more, and will likely live longer than if he/she feared death. Another important byproduct is that this person will welcome and not fear Divine Intervention in whatever form it may take, even if it is time for the Apocalypse.

The concepts in this poetry/prose book are designed to help all people build this wondrous and natural faith, and as a natural byproduct can help to significantly improve humanity's destiny. It is clear that we have problems that are becoming significantly worse. Our planet is suffering global warming (greenhouse effect) due to constantly increasing burning of hydrocarbons (fossil fuels), extinction of many species that adversely affect the food chain and that will likely adversely affect what we eat (which affects our health), major storms and climate change that is destructive to humanity, overpopulation and overusing Earth's resources, over-pollution of air, water and land, needless devastating hunger, wars and harmful conflict, tyrannous dictators in power, needless cruelty of all sorts, broken hearts, etc.

When enough people release their fear via true forgiveness, significant positive changes will take place. People will naturally begin the process of cessation of overpopulation of this planet (and lessen the overburdening of this planet's resources), stop the polluting of our air, water and land, cessation of global warming and major climate change, cessation of extinction of species vital to our welfare, elimination of wars and harmful conflict, abundance of all necessities, ending needless devastating hunger, elimination of all forms of cruelty and torture, ending of all tyrants, despots and dictators, ending of temptation into all forms of harm to any person, ending of broken hearts from a failed romance, etc.; in short, an end to all needless suffering of humanity. But this can only happen when enough people become totally committed to making this a much better world for us to live in. We're all in this together, and it is up to us to resolve our problems in an effective manner. Do we want to become extinct, or do we want to survive and increase quality of life for all of us? The future is not totally, but mostly up to us, isn't it? Your conscious and/or unconscious choice will inevitably affect all of us, including yourself and all those you care about. It is clear that we must work together to survive and flourish. If we continue to fight each other in wars, we will likely rob the future from all humanity. The outcome will be a result of the totality of humanity's mass consciousness. What will you choose to do, and will you be committed to make as big a difference as you can?

Recommended Reading

There are some books I recommend people read since you are at the end of this book, and thus should be nearly finished reading it. Not long after my spiritual awakening, I had an amazing dream. I was on a very long stairway, and each time I went up one step, the previous step mysteriously disappeared. The Holy Spirit told me the correct interpretation of that dream – that once you have made a new step in learning and experiencing spiritual growth, you will never be the same, and you will not return to the relatively unenlightened state of mind you were previously in. So, I offer that experience via the following books I am recommending.

One of the most extraordinary spiritual books I have ever read is 'A Course In Miracles', which is copyrighted by The Foundation For Inner Peace. That book also has a workbook, which brings the concepts of the text into personal experience, so I strongly recommend doing those lessons in the workbook. Miracles spontaneously began happening in my life, and became several amazing experiences and progressive movements in my soul growth as a result of doing the text and workbook at the same time.

Another book I highly recommend is 'Life After Life' by Raymond Moody. His book is about a study of people who actually died, but came back to life to tell their story, and he interviewed many of these people. The similarities of their stories and their experience with our Creator were all very similar. Their lives were generally much better after the experience, and they no longer were fearful of death, but cherished life all the more as a result.

Another book I recommend reading is 'Illusions' by Richard Bach. It is a novel, but because of the Truths in that book, it had quite a positive impact on my life.

And finally, 'The Primal Scream' by Dr. Arthur Janov (a psychiatrist) is an excellent book to help one to understand the basic concepts of how pain and trauma is formed and held in unconsciousness, how it adversely affects peoples' lives, and some insights into how to release that pain and trauma from the past. The cure for this is named Primal Therapy by the author. Some people who do Primal Therapy go through a spiritual awakening. More information about this is available at www.primaltherapy.com, and a new version of this book can be ordered from his website. I have found older versions (which I have found to be very good) can be found at www.abebooks.com.

When you are serious about your spiritual growth, you will find these books to be quite helpful. I wish you joyful and abundant soul growth, inner and outer freedom, peace, and happiness!

www.ingramcontent.com/pod-product-compliance
Lightning Source LLC
Chambersburg PA
CBHW071734040426
42446CB00012B/2353